Chino Biscontin

A friend named JESUS

The Gospel of Luke in ten stories

ST PAULS

A FRIEND NAMED JESUS
The Gospel of Luke in ten stories
Original title: *Un amico di nome Gesu*
Chino Biscontin
© 1993 Figlie di San Paolo, Milan, Italy

English edition
© 1995, ST PAULS, Homebush, Australia

Translation by Marie Therese Levey RSJ

Australian edition:
First published, October 1995
National Library of Australia
Card and ISBN number 1 875570 66 7

Illustrations:
Franca Trabacchi

Published by
ST PAULS — Society of St Paul
60-70 Broughton Road — (PO Box 230) — Homebush NSW 2140

ST PAULS
is an activity of the Priests and Brothers
of the Society of St Paul who proclaim the Gospel
through the media of social communication

Contents

Foreword

Theophilus — a person who wanted to know Jesus better

About 40 years after the death and resurrection of Jesus, a christian called Theophilus was not satisfied with what he had heard up to that time about Jesus, who did such good. He wanted to know more about him. So he was placed in contact with another christian, who was called Luke. Luke had been a faithful friend of the apostle Paul, and therefore enjoyed his trust. Many others had already turned to Luke to teach them all he knew of Jesus. So Luke decided to write a short book and give it to Theophilus with this dedication:

Dear Theophilus, there have been many accounts about Jesus written by those who knew him from the beginning. These people were eyewitnesses, and they had dedicated their lives to telling what God had done through him. Some facts which happened then already exist in the form of written stories based on their evidence. I have decided also to research all from the beginning, in order to be able to offer you an orderly account; so you yourself will know that all I have taught you is true.

We also are like Theophilus

The book written by Luke (the Gospel of the Lord Jesus according to Luke) has come down to us as well. We also, like Theophilus, can thus have precise facts about the life of Jesus.

To know about Jesus is very important and good, because he is without doubt the most wonderful man who ever lived.

The book which you have now in your hands is meant to make your first reading of the Gospel according to Luke easy for you. If you read it together with your parents, or your teacher, they will be able to give you fuller explanations that will be a great help to you. If you form part of a group of children who together want to know about Jesus, it will become even more interesting. Jesus will be better known if the Gospel is read together with those who want to know him better.

Birth and infancy of Jesus

When did Jesus live?

Luke, right at the beginning of his book, tells us in what period the facts he described took place:

In the fifteenth year of the reign of Emperor Tiberius, Pontius Pilate was governor of Judaea, and Herod was ruler of Galilee. In Jerusalem were the high priests Annas and Caiphas.

According to the calendars we have today, it would have been the year 28. Before then Jesus was almost unknown, and lived in the town called Nazareth in the region of Galilee to the north of Palestine.

A wonderful story

Luke tells of Jesus' mother and of his birth as if he were painting a beautiful picture:

God sent the Angel Gabriel to a young girl of Nazareth in Galilee called Mary. She was promised in marriage to Joseph, a descendant of King David.

The angel came to Mary and said: 'Rejoice Mary, because the Lord is with you and surrounds you with love'. Mary was afraid and wondered what the words meant. But the angel said: 'Don't be afraid, Mary. God is looking after you. Behold you will have a Son, and when he is born you will give him the name of Jesus.

PALESTINE IN THE TIME OF JESUS

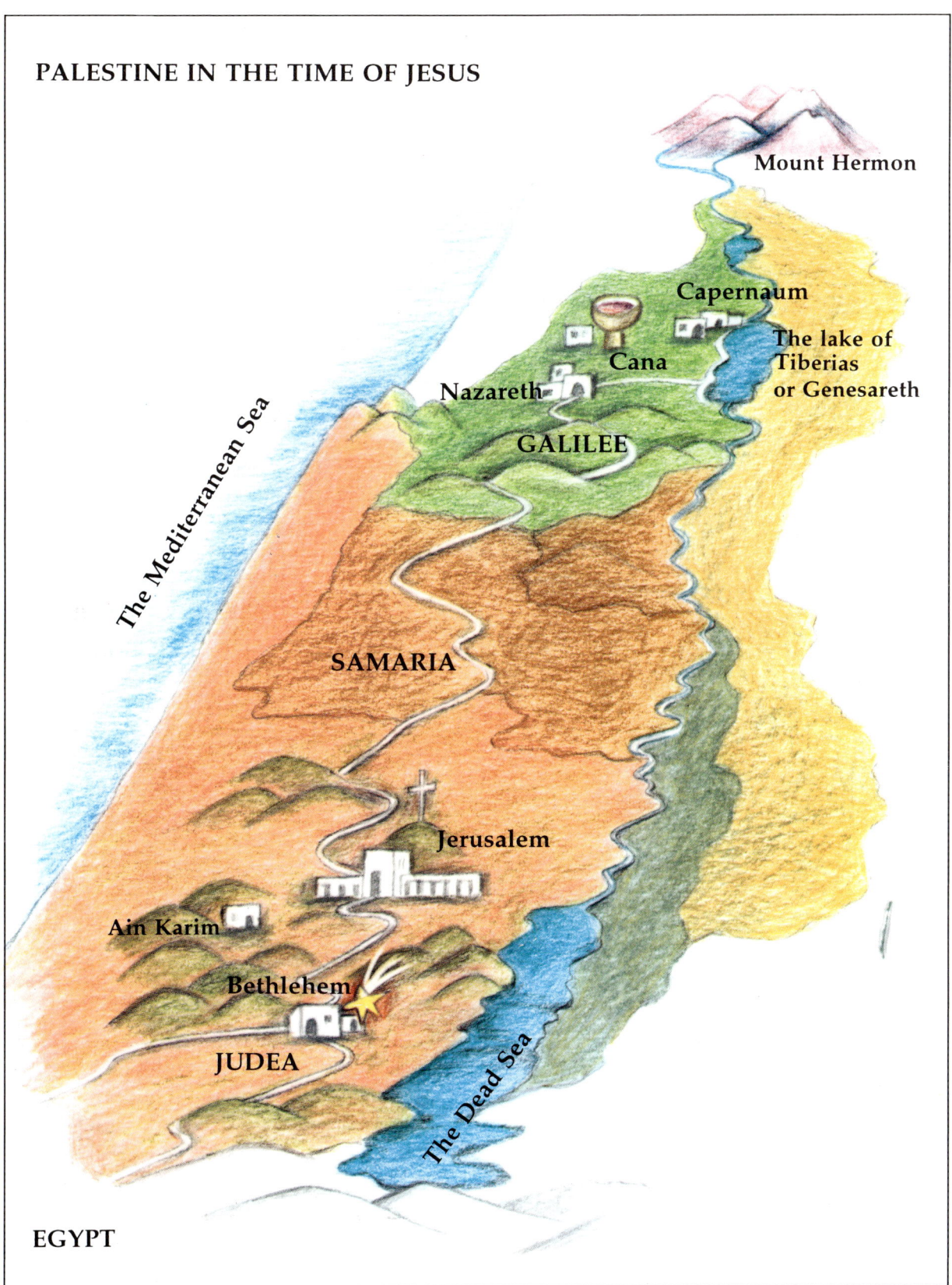

Mount Hermon

Capernaum

The lake of Tiberias or Genesareth

Cana

Nazareth

GALILEE

The Mediterranean Sea

SAMARIA

Jerusalem

Ain Karim

Bethlehem

JUDEA

The Dead Sea

EGYPT

*He will be great, and will be called Son of God and God will
fulfil in him the promises made to King David. He will be the
Lord of the descendants of Jacob and his kingdom will not end'.
Then Mary asked the angel: 'How can it be possible for me to
have a son? I am not yet married'.*

*The angel replied: 'The Holy Spirit will come down on you,
the power of God will wrap itself around you. He who will be
born of you will be the Son of the most High God'. Then Mary
said, 'I am the servant of the Lord. May it happen to me as you
have said'.*

A manger, angels, shepherds and great joy

Jesus was born in great poverty nine months after:

The Emperor Augustus sent out an order that a census be taken of all the people of the empire. Governor Quirino was responsible for Palestine. Everyone went to register in the city from which each originally came.

Joseph, together with his pregnant wife Mary, lived at Nazareth in Galilee. Joseph, being a descendant of King David, had to go to Bethlehem, which was the town of that king. They set out on the journey towards Judaea.

While they were at Bethlehem the time came for Mary to have her baby. So her son was born in that town.

Mary wrapped him up in swaddling clothes and placed him in a manger because it was not then possible to find a better place.

Nevertheless, this baby, born in such great poverty, was the one whom christians would call 'Lord, the Son of God!'

But the wise men of the time, the rich of the nearby capital Jerusalem, were not at first to know about Jesus. God wanted the poor and humble people to share in the joy of Jesus as soon as he was born:

There were in the neighbourhood of Bethlehem some shepherds who were taking care of their flocks.

An angel appeared and said to them: 'Do not be afraid. I have come to bring you great news that will fill you and all the people with joy. Today, in the town of David, is born for you the Saviour. Behold, this is how you will know him: you will find a baby wrapped in swaddling clothes and lying in a manger'.

Then many angels joined with the angel and together they sang: 'Glory to God in the heavens and peace on earth to those who love him'. As soon as the angels returned to heaven the shepherds said to each other: 'Let us go at once to Bethlehem and see what has happened, just as the Lord has told us'.

They walked quickly and found Mary and Joseph, and with them they saw the baby lying in a manger.

Since they had been able to see him, they told others what they had learned about the baby, and all those who heard them listened in wonder.

Mary, on her part, remembered all these words she had heard, and often in her heart she thought and prayed about them.

A boy blessed by God

Luke remembered also an episode which happened when Jesus was twelve years old.

Until then Jesus showed a great interest in all that concerned God:

His parents went every year to Jerusalem for the feast of the Pasch, and when Jesus was twelve years old they took him there. When the festival was over his parents prepared to return home. Jesus instead, stayed at Jerusalem, but his parents did not know this. They thought that he was in some group of the company.

After a day's walking they began to search for him among other parents and those they knew, but they could not find him. So they returned to Jerusalem.

After three days they found him in the temple, sitting with the most learned teachers, listening to them and asking them questions. All who heard marvelled that he understood such profound things and responded with such wisdom. Even his parents marvelled to see him there.

His mother said to him: 'Son, why have you done this? Your father and I have searched in agony for you'.

Jesus replied: 'Why did you look for me? Did you not know that I had to do the things of my Father? (cf. Lk 2:41-50).

Luke concludes the story of the events of Jesus' childhood:

Jesus followed his parents and returned to Nazareth with them.

He was a good and obedient child. He grew and became strong, and was loved by God and by all the people.

The great decision

A voice in the desert

Jesus stayed at Nazareth, working as a carpenter, until he was thirty years old. At thirty his life changed. He left his carpentry work and his family, and went to the villages to talk in the name of God. When and how did this change happen? Luke remembers a most important person of those times — John the Baptist. For Jesus, it was very important to meet him.

There was a man called John who lived in the desert.

God had gifted him to be able to speak in his name. John travelled along the banks of the Jordan River, inviting people to be baptised. When they allowed him to plunge them into the water, it was a sign that they had decided to change their evil way of living in order to do penance for their sins.

John spoke strongly and his words made a great impression.

To the crowds who went to be baptised by him, John cried out: 'Until now you were left to be guided by the evil spirit. Now you are worried and want to escape the condemnation of God. If it is right for you to escape, then I say to you that one thing is necessary: you must change your lives. And you must not delude yourselves by believing that you are safe because you are descendants of Abraham, the friend of God. If God wanted, he could make descendants of Abraham from these stones. I warn you: the axe is already placed at the root of these trees; every tree that does not produce good fruit will be cut down and thrown into the fire!' To the crowds who asked him, John replied: 'Whoever has two shirts must give one to whoever has none; and whoever has plenty to eat should share it with those who have none'.

Jesus receives baptism

When Jesus heard that John was speaking, he went to listen to him, and was in great admiratioin of this man. Hearing him brought the hope that truly the world would change for the better, and become more just. Jesus shared the hope that, with the help of God, the people could improve. He decided to be baptised by John and there occurred something which changed his life forever.

In the midst of the people Jesus also went forward to be baptised. While he was praying the heavens were opened, and the Holy Spirit came down in the form of a dove. A voice from heaven was heard saying: 'You are my beloved Son. My heart is full of confidence in you'.

Faith in God in a difficult situation

From then on, recalls Luke, Jesus left his work and began to speak to the people in the name of God. But before moving to this ministry he felt the need to meditate and to pray. Amongst the many ideas which sprang from his heart and turned over in his mind — which one was Jesus confident corresponded most to the will of God? Jesus made choices which were not easy, as Luke, with a dramatic story, helps us to understand. We see the entrance onto the scene of the enemy of God, the tempter:

Jesus, full of the Spirit of God, went far from the Jordan and into the desert where he stayed for forty days. There he was put to the test by the tempter.

The first temptation of Jesus concerned generosity: one can not only hold what one has for one's own advantage, but should give for the disposal of others, because this is what God wants:

For forty days he did not eat anything and at the end he was hungry. Then the tempter said to him:

'Since you are the Son of God, command this stone to become a loaf of bread for you'. Jesus replied: 'It is written in holy scripture: A person does not live only on bread'.

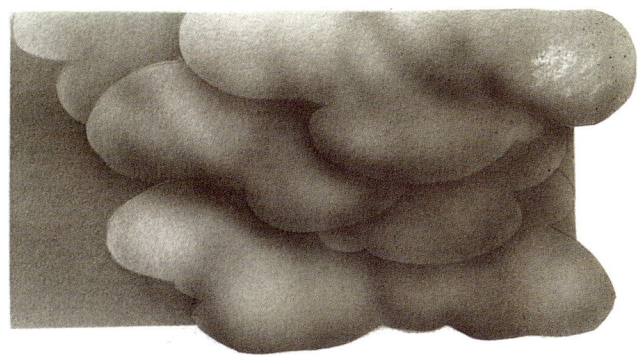

The second test was the refusal to place money above all: only God deserves the gift of our lives.

The tempter carried him on high so that in an instant he could see all the kingdoms of the earth. Then he said: 'I will give you the power and riches of these kingdoms. They are mine and I can give them to anyone I want. If you kneel before me and recognise me as your Lord all this will be yours'. Jesus replied: 'Holy scripture says: Only before God, the one Lord, do you kneel, and him alone should you adore'.

The third test was against indifference, laziness, and leaving everything to chance, against the pretence of having faith in God, so that, almost like magic, every problem will be miraculously resolved without effort.

Finally the tempter carried Jesus to Jerusalem and placed him on the highest part of the temple. He said to Jesus: 'If you are the Son of God, cast yourself down. It is written in the sacred books: God will command angels to take care of you and protect you, and also: the angels will support you with their hands, so that you will not stumble on stones'. Jesus replied: 'Holy Scripture says: Do not put God, your Lord, to the test'.

A man of decision and a tempter ambushed

Jesus remained faithful to these choices until his death, which happened about two years later.

It was not easy for him, because the tempter was always lying around waiting to catch him, like a snake ready to bite. But for Jesus, to be faithful to God and to complete the mission entrusted to him for the good of the people, was the most important thing. Nothing would have taken his path from that choice.

After having put him to the test, the tempter left him and went to wait for a more favourable occasion.

The first week of public ministry

One who was unknown becomes famous

After the baptism, records Luke, Jesus returned to Galilee strengthened by a driving enthusiasm. The people wondered and spoke even more of him amongst themselves:

Jesus returned to Galilee full of the strength that comes from the Spirit of God. He taught in the synagogues and was praised by all. He quickly became famous in all the region.

Luke gives us also an idea of how a day in the public life of Jesus unfolded:

It was the festival day and Jesus went to the synagogue and began to speak to the people. The impression he made was great because he spoke with such authority.

He succeeded in freeing those who were slaves of the evil spirit. In a violent society, full of confusion and of wickedness, the weakest were often lost and overwhelmed. Jesus gave them back peace and hope:

There was a man who had an evil spirit in him. He began to cry out: 'Enough! I know who you are: God's holy messenger! Why do you come amongst us, Jesus of Nazareth? Do you want to destroy us?' Jesus commanded the spirit: 'Be quiet, leave this man in peace and go out of him'. The evil spirit knocked that poor man to the earth, there in the middle of the group, but then left him without doing him any harm. The impression made on the people was even greater and all, amazed, asked themselves: Where does the power of this man's words come from? He commands the evil spirit and it goes away!

He even restored to health the sick who, freed, with joy gave themselves to the service of their neighbour:

Coming out of the synagogue he was invited into the house of a certain man called Simon. The mother-in-law of Simon was in bed with a very high fever. They prayed to Jesus to do something for her. He stood at her bedside and commanded the fever to go. The fever left the lady immediately, so that she was able to get up and serve them at table.

But he also gave time to prayer in order to receive light and strength from God:

The morning of the next day, before the sun had risen, Jesus retired into a desert place to pray. The people went to search him out and to find him. They all tried to persuade him not to leave them.

Jesus however said: 'I must speak of the kingdom of God in other cities also because God has entrusted me with this mission'.

The kingdom of God: This is a situation in which people do not hear any more the voice of evil, but they hear only the voice of God and they are led by him on the roads of goodness and of joy.

Jesus announced that God, on his part, provides his strength: the people must be open with trust in God to accomplish his will. The kingdom of God had brought freedom from sin and joy.

Lights and shadows on Jesus

It is not difficult to understand why the people of Capharnaum wanted to keep Jesus: he had accomplished many wonderful things. But Jesus also asked the people to be open to the will of God, to pledge themselves in the way of goodness. Also, unbelievable as it seems, little by little as the months passed, Jesus met even greater difficulties. The first problems Jesus had were with his own countrymen:

Jesus returned to Nazareth, his own village. The day of the festival, as was his custom, he went to the synagogue. He stood up to read the scriptures. Jesus read this passage from the book of the prophet Isaiah:

'The Spirit of God is on me and this is the mission for which he has sent me: to announce to the poor the good news, to proclaim freedom to prisoners and recovery of sight to the blind, to break the chains of the oppressed and to announce that it is the year of the Lord's grace'.

Having finished reading, Jesus handed the text to the attendant and sat down. All those who were there waited attentively for what he had to say. And Jesus said: 'Have you heard this passage of scripture? All that is written here is happening now'.

Jesus presented himself to his countrymen as the person of whom the great prophet Isaiah had spoken! They wondered, but they were annoyed as well: Who was this carpenter pretending to be, who until that time had lived amongst them as one of themselves?

They were amazed to hear the wonderful discourses he was able to make, and they said: But is not this the son of Joseph?

And they began to demand of him:

We have heard you speak of what was done at Capharnaum. You must do it also here, in your own country.

To such people Jesus tried to explain that jealousy and envy closed their hearts. But they were blinded by their anger:

All in the synagogue were full of indignation hearing what Jesus said.

They interrupted the assembly. They chased him out of the district, and dragged him up to the edge of a cliff.

They intended to push him over the precipice, but Jesus, passing through the midst of the crowd, went on his way.

The family of Jesus

By now Jesus could no longer live in Nazareth. He went from village to village as guest of those who befriended him in each place.

Luke tells us that unusual people began to form a group, following Jesus around.

Jesus preferred the humble and less appreciated people, like the women, children and sick. He did not mind also being with people despised, for example the tax collectors, who were thought to be swindlers and sinners because they were friends of the Romans:

One day Jesus saw a tax collector, Levi, who was seated at the table where the taxes were paid, and he said to him: 'Come you also with me'.

Jesus did not have to repeat: Levi left all and followed him. He was so happy that he prepared a great feast: those invited were also tax collectors and people like them, and Jesus accepted their invitation to table.

The pharisees and scribes, teachers of religion, said that it was truly scandalous to accept a meal with them: 'Are you not ashamed to eat and drink together with these sinners?'

But Jesus replied: 'If a doctor comes to a house, it is for the sick, and not for those who are well, that he comes. My mission is not so much for the just, but to help sinners to salvation'.

Jesus knew well who were to be his people, his family:

One day his mother and his close relatives went to find him, but they could not get near him because he was surrounded by a great crowd. Someone pointed out to him: 'Your mother and your relatives are here outside and want to see you'.

Jesus replied: 'My mother and my relatives are those who hear the word of God and put it into practice'.

A teacher by means of his life

It is the dawn of a new world

Jesus announced the kingdom which was to arise and which would bring about great changes. Luke relates some phrases of Jesus which made a great impression:

Jesus, turning to his disciples, said 'Rejoice you who are poor; because it is for you that the kingdom of God will come. Rejoice you who are hungry, because you will have food in abundance. Rejoice, you who now weep, because you will have great joy'.

For all those who had done wrong, this was truly good news. But like all news, it also found resistance from those who preferred the old situation:

Woe to those who are rich, because they will not have anyone to attend to them. Woe to those who have enough to eat now, because they will be hungry. Woe to those who now celebrate, because there will come for them days of sorrow.

A God even better than the best father

God decided that the heavenly kingdom would favour those most in need, because God is loving as the best father. God loves people as parents love their children and cares for those in need even before those who stay long hours at prayer:

Jesus said: 'When you pray, say: Father, may your name be holy, may your kingdom come. Give us this day our daily bread. Forgive us our sins as we also forgive those who do wrong against us. And let us not fall into temptation'.

And he added: 'Ask and God will hear you; those of you who search will find him, and if you knock God will not close the door on you. Listen to your father: if your son asks you for a fish, do you perhaps hand over a snake? Or if he asks you for an egg, do you hand over a scorpion?

If then you, full of defects as you are, know to give good things to your children, how much more will your Father in heaven give the Spirit to those who ask it of him'.

If God is a father, then those who want to gather into God's kingdom as loving children must be like God: the children of God must be good as God is good:

To those who listened to him Jesus said: 'You must want good even for your enemies; do good to those who hate you, praise those who speak evil of you, and pray for those who mistreat you. If anyone hits you on one cheek, turn then the other; if anyone takes your coat, do not refuse your shirt either; give to anyone who asks of you, and do not claim back whatever has been taken from you.

Do to others as you would want done to you. Love your enemies and do good to them without hope of receiving reward.

God himself will reward you, and you will be his children, because he is full of goodness even to those who are wicked and ungrateful. Be good as your Father is good. Do not judge and God will not judge you: do not condemn and God will not condemn you; forgive and God will forgive you; be generous and God will be even more so to you'.

The teaching of Jesus

Luke reported a conversation between Jesus and a scripture scholar. In a few words it is a summing up of all the teachings of Jesus:

A teacher of the law turned to him a question in order to see what he thought of it: 'Master, what must I do so that my life will not be lost?' Jesus asked him: 'What have you read in the scripture on this?'

He replied: 'You should love the Lord your God with all your heart, with all your soul, and with all your strength; and you should love your neighbour as yourself'.

And Jesus said: 'That is exactly what you must do to have eternal life'.

The scholar and the fool

Luke tells that many admired Jesus through his talks, but not all were then ready to put it into practice. Because of this Jesus spoke also with severity:

'Why do you call me "Lord, Lord!", and don't do what I tell you? I will give you an example: whoever listens to my words and obeys them — is like a person who has built a house with a strong foundation. In the rainy season the house was flooded, but it remained strong because it was well built.

On the other hand whoever hears my words but does not put them into practice is like a person who built a house without a foundation. When the floods came the house collapsed destroying all.'

Because Jesus asked people not only to listen to the good news, but also to do something about it, many retired after the first moment of enthusiasm.

Jesus continud to speak to all, but always dedicated more time to teaching the twelve disciples closest to him who believed in him.

The power of hope

Difficulties of the rich

Gradually the months passed, and difficulties increased for Jesus. The good news which Jesus taught created much enthusiasm at the beginning, but when it became clear that good deeds and a changed life were neeeded in order to receive the kingdom, there were few prepared to make such decisions and become followers. Many, then, were not pleased with the good news which Jesus brought. Luke speaks of the difficulties Jesus met, and first of all by the rich:

An important personage posed this question to Jesus: 'Master, what must I do in order to receive eternal ife?' Jesus replied: 'The commandments tell you: do not commit adultery, do not kill, do not steal, do not lie, honour your father and mother'. The man insisted: 'These things I have known and respected from my childhood'.

Then Jesus said to him: 'You still need to do one thing: sell all you possess and give the money to the poor, so that you will be rich in the eyes of God. Then come and follow me'.

At these words that man became very sad, because he was very rich. Jesus noticed his sadness and said: 'How difficult it is for a rich person to enter the kingdom of God! It is easier for a camel to pass through the eye of a needle than for a rich person to enter the kingdom of God'.

The difficulties of the pharisees and of the scribes

The most stubborn problems Jesus met, however, were those raised by the pharisees — people who were obliged to observe all the commandments and the laws prescribed by tradition, and by the scribes — the teachers of religion. They thought of God as a severe judge, ready to reward the good and punish the wicked. And in order to be faithful to this, God was regarded as a judge, who loved only the good, and scorned sinners, avoiding hearing them and being in their company.

Very different was the attitude of Jesus, who spoke of God as of a loving Father, who loved all as children, and looked for ways of saving those who made mistakes. Jesus accepted being in the company of even doubtful people.

Luke recalls one meeting of Jesus with the pharisees on these very arguments:

Near to Jesus, in order to hear him, were publicans and other outcasts of society. The pharisees and scribes grumbled: 'Look how this man makes friends of such people! And he even eats with them!'

Jesus responded by telling this story: 'There was a father who had two sons. One day the younger son said to his father: "I want my part of the inheritance".

So the father divided the inheritance between the two sons. Soon after the younger son sold his part of the property and left home.

He travelled to a distant country and spent all he possessed with a reckless life. There was a famine in that country, so he was left without anything. He did not know what to do in order to make a living. Finally he decided to look for work, and was given the job of looking after the pigs.

The famine was so great that he would have eaten even the scraps left for the pigs, but not even these were given him. Reduced to that miserable condition, he remembered his own home.

He thought: "At my father's house even the workers eat in abundance. Instead I, his son, am starving in this place". Then he made this decision: "I will return to my father and will say to him: Father, I have sinned against you and against God. I do not deserve to be called your son. Treat me as one of your hired servants".

So he got up and went towards the house.

He was still a long way off when his father saw him coming. With eyes full of tears through sorrow, the two met. The father embraced his son and covered him with kisses. The son tried to say to him: "Father, I do not deserve to be called any more your son".

But the father gave these orders to the servants: "Hurry, go and find the best garments. Put shoes on his feet and a ring on his hand. Bring the fatted calf and prepare a great feast. We will celebrate because this my son was dead and has returned to life, was lost, but now he has returned".

A great feast commenced".

Jesus stopped for an instant. Many of those who were listening were moved by the goodness of the father. But the pharisees had a cold stare. They knew that Jesus spoke of God as of a generous father and they wanted to see how he would finish the discourse. Jesus continued:

'The older brother was in the fields. On his return, when he was near the house, he heard the sounds of singing and dancing. He asked a servant who was passing what was the cause of the confusion. And the servant explained: "Your brother has returned and your father has prepared a banquet with the best calf because he is back safe and sound". The older brother was angry and absolutely refused to take part in the feast.

So his father came out to beg him to come in. But the son reproached him: "Is this fair? So many years I have worked for you and have not disobeyed your orders: yet I have never even been given a kid to celebrate with my friends. This your son wasted all that you had given him, living in this dangerous manner, yet for him you kill the best calf".

The father then said: "Son, you are always with me and all I have is also yours. But it is right to celebrate, because this your brother was dead and is now living, was lost and has been found'.

Now it was clear; the father represented God, the younger son the sinners, the older son the pharisees. And the pharisees took it very badly. They began to speak against Jesus, accusing him of being one who taught wrongly concerning how one should live one's life.

They said that he made God the figure of an unjust judge, who treated in the same way those who were good and those who were bad, and this was blasphemy. They said also that such was encouraging the evil to remain evil, and the good to give in to temptation, to become evil. Many, then, began to have doubts about Jesus and the difficulties worsened day by day.

Do not lose hope

Even the disciples of Jesus became ever more difficult. Jesus tried to show them clearly what he was asking them to be able to follow:

Jesus said: 'If one of you wants to be my disciple he must give up father, mother, wife, children, brothers and sisters and even his own life.
Whoever is not prepared to leave all to follow me, cannot be my disciple'.

And still:

'Whoever wants to save their own life will lose it, but whoever loses their own life for me, will save it'.

But Jesus invited his disciples not to let themselves be caught up by fear, but to trust in God.

To you who remained my friends I say: 'Do not fear those who kill the body, and afterwards are unable to do worse. If there is anyone to fear, it is God, because God, after you have died, has the power to cast into eternal fires.
I repeat: only God should you fear. Think about this: Cannot a pair of sparrows be bought for a few coins? Yet God does not forget even one sparrow.
You must not therefore be afraid: you are more precious to God than two little birds! He knows even how many hairs you have on your head'.

On the other hand, Jesus showed them that although many would not welcome his words, there would always be someone who listened with a sincere heart and allowed the words to bear the fruit of goodness, as happened for the seed:

The kingdom of God is like a farmer who went to sow seed in the fields. While he sowed, some grains fell along the path and was eaten by the birds.

Other seed finished on stones and, when germinated, the plants dried up because they had no moisture. Still others fell among thorns which choked the plants. But one lot of seeds fell on good soil. The plants grew and produced a hundred to one.

Above all, the poor and the humble people listened to Jesus with joy and sincerity. So in the midst of so many difficulties created by the teachers of religion, Jesus was full of hope.

Luke recalls a particular moment of Jesus' enthusiasm.

Full of joy in the Holy Spirit, Jesus exclaimed: 'How wonderful you are, Father, Lord of heaven and earth! The teachers and the wise ones refused to welcome your kingdom, and you have shown it to the humble and the simple ones'

The long journey towards the holy city

The hunt for the man

For Jesus to go preaching from village to village became more dangerous every day, as can be seen in the following story of Luke. Even the local authorities considered him to be a dangerous person and they tried to catch him:

Some noblemen came near to Jesus and said to him:
'You must get away from here: Herod is trying to find a way to kill you'.
Jesus replied: 'Go and tell that fox that for some time still I will send away the evil spirits and heal the sick. Then will come the end.
In this time which remains for me, however, I will journey on my way. It is not possible for a prophet to be taken anywhere outside of Jerusalem'.

Jesus, then, was completely aware of his mortal danger, a risk that sooner or later would become a reality:

Jesus said to his disciples:
'Don't forget what I am about to tell you — listen carefully: I am to be given over to the hands of my enemies'.

But if he had to meet death, it would be in the holy city of Jerusalem:

As the time drew near when Jesus would be taken from the earth, he made up his mind to go on to Jerusalem.
Along the way he continued to teach through the villages.

Ten healings and only one recognition

It was a very sad journey and not without humiliations and hurts, even from those who received extraordinary favours from Jesus:

During his journey towards Jerusalem, Jesus crossed Galilee and Samaria. He entered a village and was met by ten lepers. They stood at a distance and cried out: 'Jesus, Master, have pity on us'. Noticing them, Jesus said: 'Go and show yourselves to the priests'. And as they went they were healed.

One of them, when he saw that he was healed, turned around full of gratitude that God had made him well. He found Jesus and threw himself on his knees and did not stop thanking him. The man was a Samaritan.

Jesus observed with disappointment: 'Were there not ten healed? Where are the other nine? Only this stranger has returned to render glory to God!' And to the leper he said: 'Get up and go. Your faith has saved you'.

A tricky welcome

There were those who welcomed Jesus during his journey. But it was necessary to keep one's eyes open: not all were friendly.

A pharisee invited him to eat at his house. Jesus entered and sat at table. The pharisee noticed with wonder that he had not observed the religious custom of washing his hands.

Then Jesus said bravely: 'You pharisees worry about cleaning the outside of the cups and the plates, but you are not so concerned that what is inside contains injustice and violence. How foolish are your ways! Do you not realise that God created the inside? If you want to please God as you should, I will tell you what you must do: share your food with the poor'. And he left that house.

A dangerous welcome but full of joy

The pharisees by now looked for Jesus only to find ways to trap him, and catch him in speech or in actions so that they could denounce him. It was actually a person despised by the pharisees, a public sinner, who made Jesus welcome, opening not only his house but also his heart:

Jesus reached Jericho and was passing through that city.

A certain Zacchaeus, a rich leader of the publicans, tried to find Jesus, but was unable to do so in the crowd because he was short. So he ran ahead and climbed up into a sycamore tree which was growing along the side of the road. When Jesus arrived at the place, he looked up to see him and said: 'Zacchaeus, come down because today I will stay at your house'.

Zacchaeus hurriedly climbed down and received Jesus with joy.

Seeing this those present were grumbling against Jesus because he had accepted the hospitality of a sinner.

In the house of Zacchaeus, however, everything was beautiful: Jesus was given the first place at the table and Zacchaeus said to Jesus: 'Lord, I have decided to give half of my possessions to the poor. And if I have cheated anyone I will restore it four times over'.

And Jesus said: 'Today salvation has come to this house. Is not this our brother? I have come to search and save those who are lost'.

A loving welcome

Jesus also had some friends, however, who remained faithful to him, and he went into their houses and was treated with loving trust:

Jesus entered a village and was welcomed into the house of a woman called Martha. Her sister, Mary, stayed listening to Jesus, sitting at his feet, while Martha was busy preparing adequate welcome. At a certain moment Martha said to Jesus: 'Lord, does it not matter to you that my sister leaves me alone to do all the work?'

Jesus replied: 'Martha, Martha, you worry yourself about many things when little matters. There is only one thing which you cannot do without. Mary has chosen the better part and it will not be taken from her'.

It was not yet time to think about a splendid meal. Other more important concerns of the heart had to be attended to, and above all that of listening to Jesus in order to stay faithful even in the terrible storm which by now was coming close.

For the third time Jesus said to the disciples: 'Behold, we go to Jerusalem and all will happen which the prophets have said. I will be given over to strangers, tortured, humiliated and covered with spittle. After they have whipped me, they will kill me. The third day I will rise'.

They did not understand any of these words of Jesus which appeared to them impossible.

At Jerusalem

Even the stones will cry out

In these last days Jesus had lived almost by hiding. When he arrived at Jerusalem, the holy city was full of people who had come from every part to celebrate the feast of the Passover.

Many were happy to see Jesus, and amongst these also were the children. Luke records:

When Jesus came close to Bethphage and Bethany, on the hill of the Mount of Olives, he sent ahead two of his disciples: 'Go into the house which is ahead of us. Entering in you will find a little donkey on which no one has yet ridden. Untie it and bring it here' (cf. Lk 19:29-30).

They brought the donkey, put their cloaks over its back, and helped Jesus on. They spread other cloaks on the road, and gradually he advanced. Along the descent of the Mount of Olives the disciples, with joy and with loud voices, began to praise God for all that had been seen in Jesus. They cried out: 'May the king live long who comes in the name of the Lord! Peace in the heavens and glory to God'.

Some pharisees, drawing near to Jesus in the midst of the crowds, said to him: 'Master, command your disciples to be quiet'. But he replied: 'If they are quiet, the stones will cry out'

Hearts harder than stones

That squabble with the pharisees was only the beginning of the final encounter which, in Jerusalem, Jesus would have with those who opposed his preaching and his work. Jesus was aware of it:

When he was within sight of the city, Jesus began to weep and said: 'Jerusalem, Jerusalem, you kill the prophets and throw stones at God's messengers; how many times I have tried to gather together your people, as a hen gathers her brood, but you did not want it! Ah, if even you today had known about the road to peace! But your eyes are blinded'.

At Jerusalem Jesus openly attacked the falsehood of the pharisees and of their scribes:

Woe to you, pharisees, who pay promptly all your offerings as the law requires, but then do not show justice or the love of God.
Woe to you who are like unmarked tombs on which the people walk without noticing it.
And woe to you, teachers of the law, who burden with impossible loads those who listen, with all your traditions and prescriptions, and you do not stretch a finger to assist those who carry the loads! Woe to you, who claim to be the ones to have in your hands the keys to the path of God: you have prevented those who wanted to enter'.

Chasing the robbers of the house of God!

These last words of Jesus help us to understand an act of astonishing bravery which he performed in the temple. According to Jesus, the temple, which was the house of God, was held captive by those who had not entered into the friendship of God and who prevented others from doing it also.

Jesus went to the temple and went in. He began to drive out all the sellers he found there, crying out: 'God has said: My house will be the house of prayer for all. You instead treat it as a house of thieves!'

Jesus, betrayed, gives his life

Now against Jesus were all the authorities, and their hatred was brimming over:

The high priests, the scribes and the other authorities looked for a way to kill him.
They did not know how they would do it, because Jesus had many followers amongst those who heard him.

It was not possible to arrest Jesus amongst the crowds during the day. And in the evening, when the crowd withdrew, Jesus hid in a cave in the Mount of Olives. Then the authorities looked around for one who, for money, would show the hiding place of Jesus. Luke describes a very sad episode: a close friend of Jesus betrayed him:

The evil spirit entered into Judas Iscariot, one of the twelve apostles. He went to the high priests and the guards concerning the way he could deliver Jesus into their hands. They were very pleased at this unexpected help and offered to pay him money. Judas accepted, and from that moment he waited for an opportunity to hand Jesus over to them.

The fate of Jesus was now sealed: it was only a question of hours. He had nothing else but his own life. It was a thought that never left him. This can be understood from this episode:

He happened to notice some rich people who threw their offering into the treasure chest in the temple. He saw also a poor widow who threw in a pair of coins. Jesus commented:. 'This widow, poor as she is, has made the greatest offering. The rich give what they have to spare; she instead, in her poverty, has given all she had to live on'.

Not to give something, but to give one's own life: this was the greatest sign of generosity, of love: it was what Jesus would accomplish.

The night in which Jesus was betrayed

The last supper of Jesus

Luke kept the precious record for us of the last hours of Jesus' life. At Jerusalem there was a festal feeling for the greatest feast for the Jews, the Passover.

The day came when, according to tradition, the meal with the lamb was held for the feast of the Passover. Jesus sent Peter and John to Jerusalem with this instruction: 'Go and prepare what is necessary so that we can celebrate the Paschal meal'. They went and made the preparation.

When it was the time, Jesus took his place at table together with the apostles and said: 'I have wanted so much to be able to eat the Paschal meal with you before I suffer and die. It is my last Passover. It will find fulfilment in the kingdom of God'.

And, according to custom, he took first the chalice of wine, recited the prayer of thanksgiving and said: 'Pass this around to each other. It is the last wine that I drink. The kingdom of God will come' (cf. Lk 22:7-16).

Jesus took his place as head at the table of the Jewish Passover. But he used new words: from these one can understand the meaning that Jesus gave to his death. He remained faithful to God even after all, as well as completing the mission to which God had entrusted him.

He was ready to give his life so that between God and all people was a new relation, a new alliance, made of forgiveness, of trust, of love:

After passing first the wine, Jesus took the loaf of bread in his hands, recited the prayer of thanksgiving, then broke it and distributed it amongst all saying: 'This is my body which is given for you. Do this in memory of me'. At the end of the meal he took the chalice of wine and said: 'This chalice is the new alliance in my blood, which comes for you'.

A God who pardons

Then Jesus turned to his disciples with words of love and comfort, so that they would never lose confidence in the fact that God forgives those who sin, and desires a close and loving communion with all his children:

Jesus said: 'Simon, Simon, the evil spirit puts you to the extreme test. I have prayed for you, so that your faith will not fail. When you rise up again, you must give strength to your brothers. You,' he remarked, 'remained near me even in the middle of difficulties. It is for you that I prepare a house as the Father prepared it for me. You will eat and drink at my table in my house and you will be given great honour. You will have authority over the people of God, the twelve tribes of Israel'.

But Jesus wanted them to understand that to have authority did not mean to want to be overbearing. God wants us to be brothers and sisters and whoever has more must give it for the service of others.

Amongst the disciples a discussion arose concerning who would hold the most important place in the kingdom. But Jesus corrected them: 'There are kings who have power and so exercise authority amongst their people. For this they are called friends of the people. But amongst you it is the opposite: the greatest must take the last place, and whoever wants to command must first learn to serve'.

Alone, face to face with death

Jesus could well speak thus: he had come to serve in the midst of them. Moreover, he had given his very life. The apostles were confused, and did not understand very well. Only after the resurrection of Jesus would they begin to understand.

Now Jesus was truly alone facing his imminent death. But he knew God would not abandon him:

Jesus, accompanied by his disciples, went into a lonely place on the Mount of Olives. When he reached there, he said to them: 'Pray that you will not fail, because it is the moment of the trial'. Then he went away from them a little and on his knees he prayed: 'Father, if it is possible, take away from me the cup of suffering which falls to me. However, your will be done, not mine'. As he prayed more intensely the agony overtook him. His sweat was like drops of blood that fell to the earth. Rising up, he went to his disciples. He found them asleep, overcome by tiredness. He woke them and said: 'Why do you sleep? Rise up and pray so that the temptation will not overcome you'.

Arrested like a dangerous lawbreaker

Not all the apostles were asleep: one, unfortunately, stayed very much awake.

Jesus had not yet finished speaking when a crowd arrived. Judas, one of the twelve, was leading them. He drew near to Jesus and saluted him with a kiss. Jesus said to him: 'Judas, do you betray me with a kiss!' Then he turned to those who were with him, high priests, officials of the guard and other authorities: 'You are armed with spades and clubs as if I were a brigand. Yet I was every day in the temple and you did not arrest me. But this is the hour you choose, the hour of darkness'. They grasped him, took him away and led him to the house of the high priest.

The other apostles ran away, abandoning Jesus. And Peter, who later tried to mix amongst the servants and soldiers in the courtyard of the house of the high priests, covered by a servant, swore that he had never known Jesus! It was truly the hour of darkness, of cruelty and wickedness:

Meanwhile those who were guarding Jesus made fun and tormented him. Covering his eyes, they mocked him and then asked him: 'Tell us, O prophet, guess who it is that struck you!'

And they insulted him in many other ways.

Nailed to a cross and killed

Condemned by a religious tribunal

Jesus was first judged by a tribunal of the people's authorities. He was accused, as we have just seen, of teaching a new doctrine, false and dangerous, in the name of God. The authorities wanted verified, in a solemn and definite manner, if Jesus still claimed to have taught those things in the name of God.

When it was daylight, he was brought to members of the Jewish tribunal. Jesus was brought into the council hall. The questioning began at once: 'If you are the one sent by God, tell us now openly'.

Jesus replied: 'Even if I tell you, you will not believe me, and if I put questions to you will not answer me. But from now on I will sit next to God and will have his authority'. At these words they exclaimed: 'Well then, you claim to be the Son of God!' He replied: 'It is as you have said: I am he'.

Then they began to cry out: 'Why is there need to continue questioning in order to have proof? Now we have it from his own lips'.

Condemned by the Roman governor

Now it was necessary to convince the Roman governor that Jesus deserved to be killed: only the Roman authority could approve capital punishment.

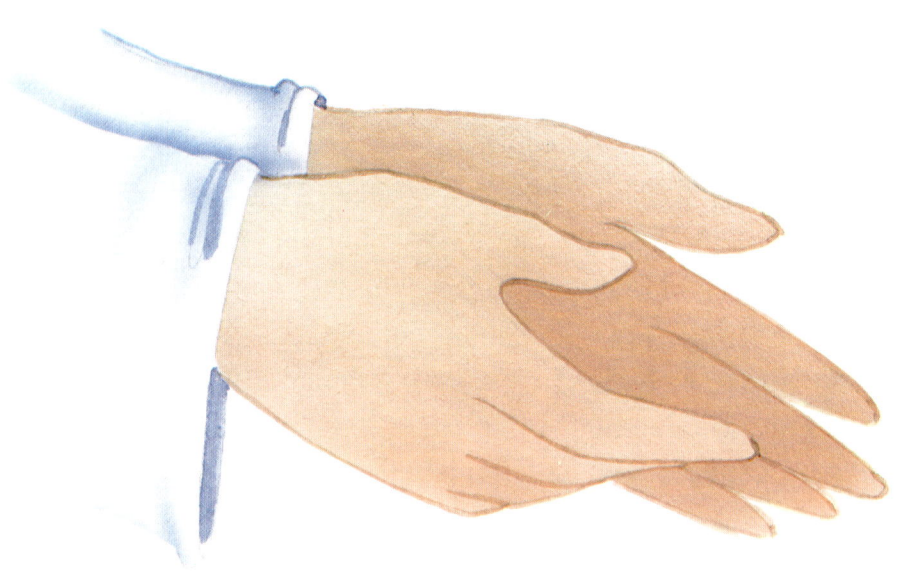

All of the assembly of the authorities rose up and Jesus was transferred to the presence of Pilate. They presented Jesus to him with these accusations: 'We have the proofs that this person instigated the people to revolt, taught them not to pay taxes to the Emperor and went around claiming to be king of the Jews'. Pilate asked him: 'Is it true that you claim to be the king of the Jews?' He replied: 'You say that it is so'.

Pilate turned to the authorities: 'It does not appear to me that this man has done anything wrong, as you have said'. But they said instead: 'He is a rebel. He stirred up the people against Judea, after having travelled through Galilee'.

But Pilate retorted to the authorities: 'You have presented this man to me as an agitator; I have questioned him, as you have seen, but I find nothing criminal in that of which he has been accused. According to me he has done nothing which deserves the death sentence. I will have him scourged, then let him go free'. But those present called out: 'To death, to death'.

Pilate, who wanted to free Jesus, tried to insist, but those present cried out even more: 'To the cross, to the cross!' For the third time he tried to convince them: 'But what evil has he done? I find no fault and will not condemn him. I will give him a severe beating and then let me go'. They however, insisted to such an extent that he should be condemned to crucifixion, and their cry became all the time more threatening.

Pilate, at the end, had to give in, and abandoned Jesus into their hands.

Nailed to a cross he continues to save

The enemies of Jesus were victorious, and Jesus was condemned to the death of those who rebelled against the Romans: crucifixion.

They took Jesus and brought him to the place of execution. They pressed a certain Simon of Cyrene to carry the cross beside him. Together with Jesus came two robbers to be judged. They reached a place called 'the Skull'. There Jesus was nailed to the cross and with him also the two thieves, one at his right and the other at his left. Jesus from the cross prayed: 'Father forgive them, for they do not know what they are doing'.

Even from the cross Jesus forgave and continued his mission of saving:

One of the two robbers crucified with him insulted him: 'You who pretend to be the messenger of God, save yourself and us too'. But the other reproved him: 'You, like him, are so near death and have not regard for God. If we are condemned, at least there was a reason; he instead, has not done anything wrong'.

Then he added: 'Jesus, remember me when you enter your kingdom'. And Jesus replied to him: 'Today you will be with me in paradise'.

Trust in God to the last

The hour came in which Jesus was to give his life: he had trusted in God and had loved all people to the last extreme.

Towards midday the sun was eclipsed and darkness descended over the earth until three hours later. In the temple, the veil which separated the people from the presence of God, was torn in the middle from the ceiling to the floor.

At that hour Jesus cried out: 'Father, into your hands I entrust my life'. Having said this, he expired. The commander of the guard, seeing what had happened in the presence of God, with great frankness, exclaimed: 'This man was just'. Even those who had been watching, dumbfounded, returned to the city beating their breasts.

Buried with love as seed in the earth

To the friends of Jesus there was nothing left but to bury his body with love.

A man by the name of Joseph of Arimathea, a good and upright person, member of the council (but he had no part of the decisions of others), was one of those who waited for the kingdom of God.

Bravely he went to Pilate and asked to be allowed to bury the body of Jesus. He lowered it from the cross, wrapped it in linen and placed it in a tomb dug out of rock in which no one yet had been buried.

It was the vigil of the Passover and already, according to custom, people came with torches. The women who had come with Jesus from Galilee, followed Joseph and were able to see where the tomb was and how the body of Jesus had been placed.

They returned and prepared ointments and spices. The day after, however, they had to respect the law of sacred rest.

He walks still with us and sits at our table

Do not look amongst the dead for one who is alive

Jesus trusted in God, and whoever trusts in God will not be disappointed. The tomb held the body of Jesus, but the great hands of God had gathered together his life. As a seed germinates in the earth, Jesus was raised up by God.

Luke narrates what happened the morning of the Passover.

The Sabbath day over, the day after, early in the morning, the women who had followed Jesus from Galilee to the tomb, returned to the burial place carrying with them the perfume which had been prepared according to custom. When they arrived at the place they found the stone, which closed the tomb, rolled away. They entered, and behold the body of Jesus was not there. As they stood there they did not know what to think.

Suddenly there appeared near to them two men with shining clothes. The women, frightened, bowed their heads to the ground. However, the men said to them: 'Why are you looking amongst the dead for one who is living? He is not here, he is risen. Remember his words, when he was in Galilee: he told you that he would be given into the hands of sinners, that he would be killed and that he would rise on the third day'. They remembered those words and, returned quickly from the sepulchre, going to announce everything to the eleven and all the others. The women were Mary of Magdala, Joanna, Mary the mother of James, and others. To the apostles these words seemed unbelievable and they thought that the women imagined it.

Peter, however, ran to the sepulchre and, looking in, saw that there were only the cloths with which the body of Jesus had been wrapped. He did not know what to think and returned home wondering.

He is recognised breaking the bread

Death had not imprisoned Jesus. If one wants to find Jesus, it is not amongst the dead that he is found. He is living and can be met even today.

Remember this beautiful story about him recounted by Luke:

On that same day two disciples were travelling towards the village of Emmaus, about twelve kilometres from Jerusalem. While walking they spoke together about the things which had happened in those days. While they talked, Jesus in person, met them and walked with them. They, however, did not recognise Jesus. He asked them: 'What happenings are you talking about?'

They stopped and looked at him with eyes full of sadness. One of them, Cleophas, exclaimed: 'You must be a stranger if you do not know of what happened at Jerusalem in these days'. He demanded: 'What things?'

They responded: 'All that happened to Jesus of Nazareth. He was a prophet, great in deed and word before God and all people. Our high priests and our authorities, however, condemned him to the Romans and so they killed him on a cross. We hoped that the liberation of our people would come through him, instead already three days have passed since his death. To tell the truth, some women of our group amazed us. They went to the sepulchre and not finding his body, they were returning, but had a vision of angels, who affirmed he is alive. Some of our companions have gone to the tomb and have found it as the women said, but have not seen him'.

Then he said to them: 'How slow you are in your hearts to understand! Have the prophets not spoken clearly? Was it not necessary for the Messiah of God to undergo suffering before entering into the glory of God?' And, beginning with the scriptures of Moses, through the prophets, he explained to them all that referred to him.

Meanwhile they arrived at Emmaus, and he acted as if he were going on. The two disciples said instead: 'The day is now almost over and darkness approaches; stay with us'. He accepted their hospitality.

When he was seated at the table, Jesus took the bread, recited the prayer of thanksgiving, broke and distributed the bread. Then their eyes were opened and they remembered.

Jesus disappeared from their sight. They, recovering from their stupor, said to each other: 'Were not our hearts burning in our breasts while, walking with us on the road, he explained the scriptures?' And they returned to Jerusalem. There they found the eleven gathered together with others who said to them: 'Truly the Lord is risen and appeared to Simon'.

Then they told what had happened to them on the road and how they had recognised him in the breaking of bread.

We also then, can meet Jesus, on our roads, in our homes, in the church. When people come together to find hope, and to understand the will of God, Jesus is with them. When families open their homes in welcome, when they share bread as a sign of solidarity with the poor, Jesus is there. When we pray together in church, on Sundays, and listen to the readings, and celebrate the Eucharist of the Lord, Jesus is living with us, and he helps us to walk through life following the path which he, in his goodness, has left on this our earth.